MW00697369

PLAYMAKERS IN S
BILINGUAL

The
PITCHER
El lanzador

by Madison Capitano
and Pablo de la Vega

Rourke
Educational Media

A Division of
Carson
Dellosa
Education
rourkeeducationalmedia.com

BEFORE AND DURING READING ACTIVITIES

Before Reading: *Building Background Knowledge and Vocabulary*

Building background knowledge can help children process new information and build upon what they already know. Before reading a book, it is important to tap into what children already know about the topic. This will help them develop their vocabulary and increase their reading comprehension.

Questions and Activities to Build Background Knowledge:

1. Look at the front cover of the book and read the title. What do you think this book will be about?
2. What do you already know about this topic?
3. Take a book walk and skim the pages. Look at the table of contents, photographs, captions, and bold words. Did these text features give you any information or predictions about what you will read in this book?

Vocabulary: *Vocabulary Is Key to Reading Comprehension*

Use the following directions to prompt a conversation about each word.

- Read the vocabulary words.
- What comes to mind when you see each word?
- What do you think each word means?

Vocabulary Words:		Palabras del vocabulario	
• curveballs	• stealing	• bolas curvas	• ponche
• fastballs	• strike zone	• bolas rectas	• robar
• pitching rubber	• strikeout	• plato del lanzador	• zona de strike

During Reading: *Reading for Meaning and Understanding*

To achieve deep comprehension of a book, children are encouraged to use close reading strategies. During reading, it is important to have children stop and make connections. These connections result in deeper analysis and understanding of a book.

 Close Reading a Text

During reading, have children stop and talk about the following:

- Any confusing parts
- Any unknown words
- Text to text, text to self, text to world connections
- The main idea in each chapter or heading

Encourage children to use context clues to determine the meaning of any unknown words. These strategies will help children learn to analyze the text more thoroughly as they read.

When you are finished reading this book, turn to the next-to-last page for **After Reading Questions** and an **Activity**.

Table of Contents

The Pitcher 5

The Pitcher's Skills 13

So You Want to Be a Pitcher? 22

Memory Game 30

Index 31

After Reading Questions .31

Activity 31

About the Authors 32

Índice

El lanzador 5

Las habilidades del lanzador 13

¿Así que quieres ser lanzador? 22

Juego de memoria 30

Índice analítico 31

Preguntas posteriores a la lectura 31

Actividad 31

Sobre los autores 32

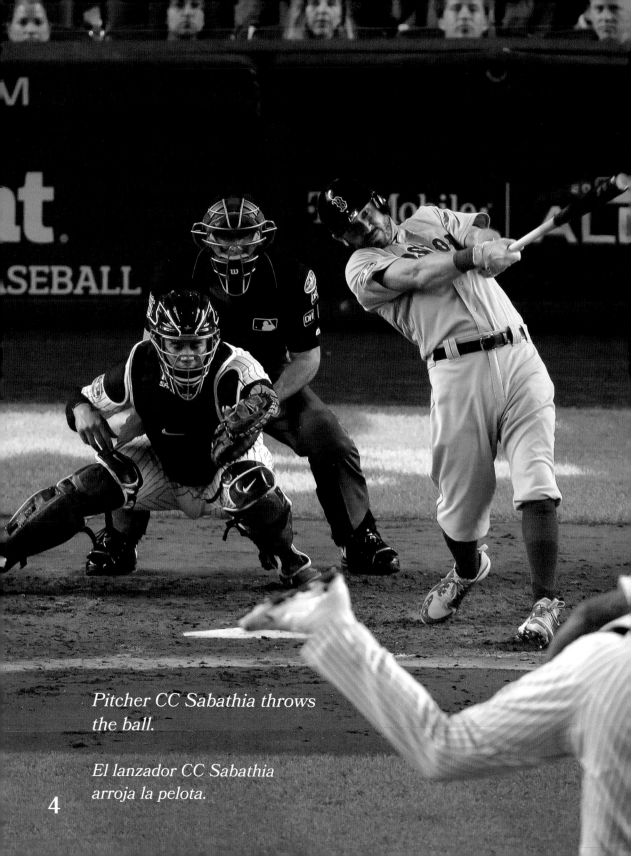

Pitcher CC Sabathia throws
the ball.

El lanzador CC Sabathia
arroja la pelota.

The Pitcher

The pitcher throws the ball to batters on the other team. The batters try to hit the ball with a bat. A good pitcher makes the difference between winning and losing a game.

- - - - - - - - - - -

El lanzador

El lanzador arroja la pelota a los bateadores del otro equipo. Los bateadores intentan golpear la pelota con un bat. Un buen lanzador puede hacer la diferencia entre ganar o perder un juego.

A pitcher tries to throw the ball into a small area called the **strike zone**. Pitches outside the strike zone are called balls. Four balls means the batter walks to first base.

strike zone (strike zohn): area over home plate that a pitch must pass to be a strike

— — — — — — — — — —

Un lanzador intenta arrojar la pelota dentro de un campo pequeño llamado **zona de strike**. Los lanzamientos que caen fuera de la zona de strike son llamados bolas. Después de cuatro bolas el bateador puede caminar a la primera base.

zona de strike (zona de straic): área arriba del plato por la que un lanzamiento debe pasar para hacer un strike

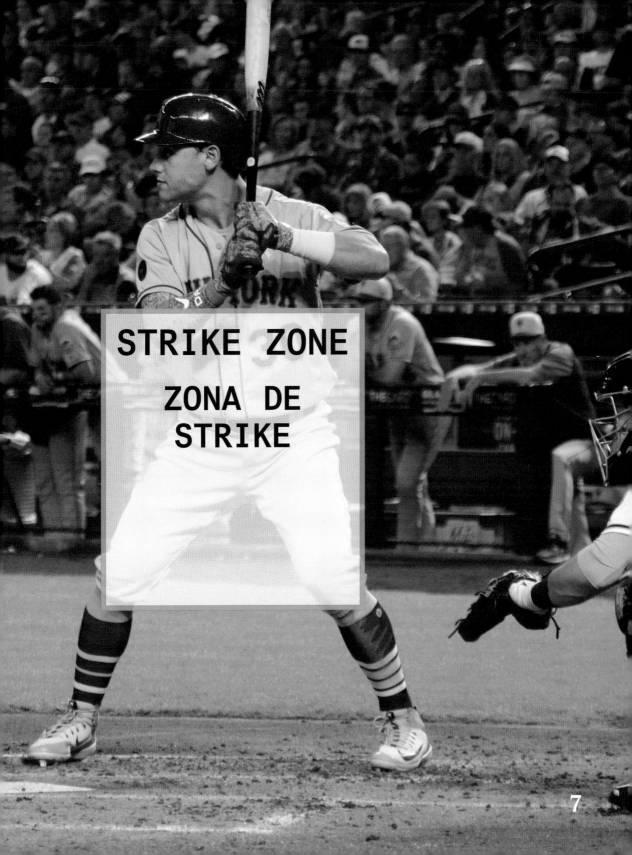

STRIKE ZONE

ZONA DE STRIKE

A pitcher throws from a mound on the field. The pitching motion is called a wind-up. The pitcher's foot must touch the **pitching rubber**.

pitching rubber (PICH-ing RUHB-ur): a white, rubber rectangle on the pitcher's mound

— — — — — — — — — — — —

Un lanzador arroja la pelota desde un montículo en el campo. El movimiento previo es llamado preparación para el lanzamiento. El pie del lanzador debe tocar el **plato del lanzador**.

plato del lanzador: un rectángulo blanco y de hule que está en el montículo del lanzador

Pitcher Peter Lambert prepares to throw the ball.

El lanzador Peter Lambert se prepara para arrojar la pelota.

There are starting pitchers and relief pitchers. A starting pitcher is a team's first pitcher in a game. A relief pitcher comes in when the starting pitcher is tired or hurt.

— — — — — — — — — —

Hay lanzadores abridores y relevistas. Un lanzador abridor es el primer lanzador del equipo durante un juego. Un lanzador relevista llega cuando el lanzador abridor se cansa o lastima.

Starting pitcher Adam Wainwright (left) and closing pitcher ▶ *Carlos Martinez (right) talk after a win.*

El lanzador abridor Adam Wainwright (izquierda) y el lanzador cerrador Carlos Martínez (derecha) conversan después de un triunfo.

Bring It Home

A *closer* is a relief pitcher who only plays during the ninth inning. They protect their team's lead.

Hasta el final

Un *cerrador* es un lanzador relevista que sólo juega durante la novena entrada. Cuidan de la ventaja del equipo.

Pitcher Jennie Finch winds up.

La lanzadora Jennie Finch se prepara para lanzar.

The Pitcher's Skills

A pitcher must have a good arm. This means they can throw the ball hard. Many pitchers throw at least 85 to 100 pitches in one game.

– – – – – – – – – –

Las habilidades del lanzador

Un lanzador debe tener un buen brazo. Esto significa que pueden arrojar la pelota con fuerza. Muchos lanzadores hacen al menos de 85 a 100 lanzamientos por juego.

Good pitchers throw the ball very fast. Some pitchers do not throw as fast as others. They focus on aim. A careful pitcher can get a **strikeout**!

strikeout (STRIKE-out): an out called when a batter has three strikes

— — — — — — — — — — —

Los buenos lanzadores arrojan la pelota muy rápido. Algunos lanzadores no la arrojan tan rápido como otros. Se enfocan en un objetivo. ¡Un lanzador cuidadoso puede lograr un **ponche**!

ponche: un *out* cuando el bateador hace tres strikes

S 5562

000402Z

0004025562

Inspected By: Maria_Salinas

Sell your books at sellbackyourBook.com! Go to sellbackyourBook.com and get an instant price quote. We even pay the shipping - see what your old books are worth today!

The umpire calls a strikeout.

El árbitro marca un ponche.

15

There are many different pitches. **Curveballs** and screwballs trick the batter.

curveballs (kurv-BAWLS): pitches that spin away from their path as they get close to the batter

– – – – – – – – – – –

Hay muchas formas distintas de lanzamientos. La **bolas curvas** y las de tirabuzón engañan al bateador.

bolas curvas: lanzamientos que se alejan de su trayectoria conforme se acercan al bateador

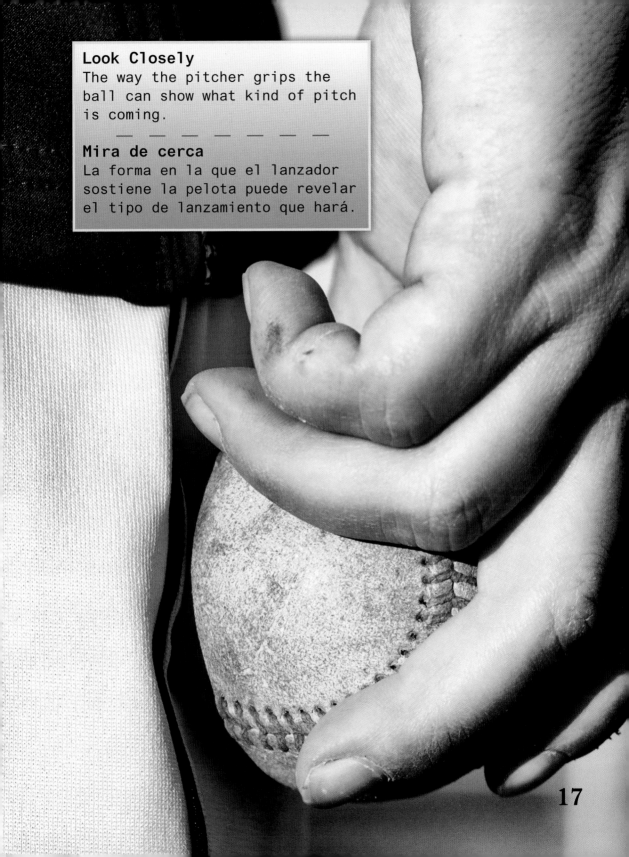

Look Closely
The way the pitcher grips the ball can show what kind of pitch is coming.

— — — — — — —

Mira de cerca
La forma en la que el lanzador sostiene la pelota puede revelar el tipo de lanzamiento que hará.

17

Fastballs whiz right by the batter. Professional pitchers throw fastballs that are faster than a cheetah!

fastballs (fast-BAWLS): pitches thrown at or near a pitcher's top speed

- - - - - - - - - - -

Las **bolas rectas** pasan volando al bateador. ¡Los lanzadores profesionales tiran rectas más rápidas que una chita!

bolas rectas: un lanzamiento a la velocidad máxima o cerca de la velocidad máxima del lanzador

Batter Pedro Florimón misses the fastball.

El bateador Pedro Florimón falla al tratar de golpear una bola recta.

Blink and You'll Miss It
A pitch of 100 miles (160.9 kilometers) per hour can get to the batter in less than half a second!

Parpadea y no lo verás
¡Un lanzamiento a 100 millas (160.9 kilómetros) por hora puede llegar al bateador en menos de medio seguno!

A pitcher must also field their position. They keep runners from **stealing** bases. They must pay attention.

stealing (STEEL-ing): when a player on base tries to run to the next base before their teammate has hit the ball

— — — — — — — — — — —

Un lanzador debe poder también mantener su posición. Evitan que los corredores se **roben** bases. Deben estar atentos.

robar: cuando un jugador en una base trata de correr a la siguiente antes de que batee su compañero

Pitcher Tyler Skaggs tags out a player ▶ *attempting to steal a base.*

El lanzador Tyler Skaggs atrapa a un jugador que intentaba robarse una base.

So You Want to Be a Pitcher?

Pitchers come in many shapes and sizes. Most professional pitchers are taller than the average person, but not all pitchers are tall.

— — — — — — — — — —

¿Así que quieres ser un lanzador?

Hay lanzadores de todos tipos y tamaños. La mayoría de los lanzadores profesionales son más altos que el común de las personas, pero no todos.

Pitcher Daniel Herrera is 5 foot 6 inches (167.6 centimeters) tall.

El lanzador Daniel Herrera mide 5 pies con 6 pulgadas (167.6 centímetros) de altura.

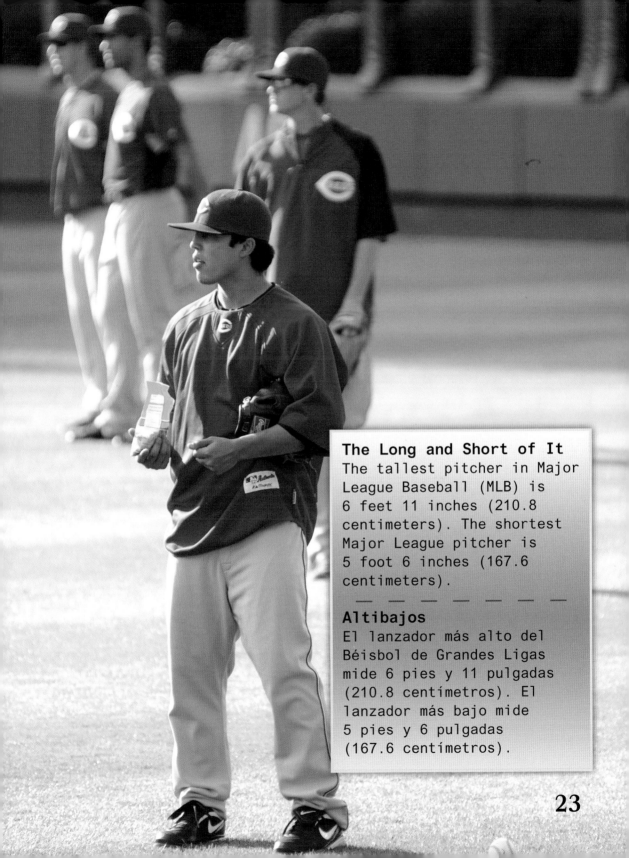

The Long and Short of It
The tallest pitcher in Major League Baseball (MLB) is 6 feet 11 inches (210.8 centimeters). The shortest Major League pitcher is 5 foot 6 inches (167.6 centimeters).

— — — — — — — —

Altibajos
El lanzador más alto del Béisbol de Grandes Ligas mide 6 pies y 11 pulgadas (210.8 centímetros). El lanzador más bajo mide 5 pies y 6 pulgadas (167.6 centímetros).

Pitchers can be left-handed or right-handed. Left-handed pitchers are called southpaws.

— — — — — — — — — —

Los lanzadores pueden ser diestros o zurdos. A los lanzadores zurdos también se les puede decir zocatos.

In the Details
Pitchers train a lot. They train their arms, legs, and shoulders. They train to be strong and flexible.

— — — — — — —

Ahí está el detalle
Los lanzadores entrenan mucho. Entrenan los brazos, las piernas y los hombros. Entrenan para ser los mejores.

Left-handed pitcher Cat Osterman
steps up to the plate.

La lanzadora zurda Cat Osterman se
coloca en el plato.

A good pitcher shows leadership on the field. They must be a good teammate.

– – – – – – – – – – –

Un buen lanzador muestra su liderazgo en el campo. Deben ser buenos compañeros de equipo.

Pitcher German Marquez (far right) ▷
meets with his teammates.

El lanzador Germán Márquez (extrema derecha) se reúne con sus compañeros.

27

Pitchers are an important part of a team. If you love baseball or softball and think you could be a good leader, then start practicing! You might make a great pitcher.

— — — — — — — — — —

Los lanzadores son parte importante del equipo. Si te encanta el béisbol o el sóftbol y piensas que puedes ser un buen líder, ¡comienza a practicar! Podrías convertirte en un gran lanzador.

Memory Game / Juego de memoria

Look at the pictures. What do you remember reading on the pages where each image appeared?

– –

Mira las imágenes. ¿Qué recuerdas haber leído en las páginas donde aparece cada imagen?